21st Century Skills INNOVATION Library

Vaccines

by Judy Alter

Published in the United States of America by Cherry Lake Publishing
Ann Arbor, Michigan
www.cherrylakepublishing.com

Content Adviser: Noshene Ranjbar, MD

Design: The Design Lab

Photo Credits: Cover and page 3, ©iStockphoto.com/kkgas; page 4, ©iStockphoto.com/
ozgurdonmaz; page 6, ©North Wind Picture Archives/Alamy; page 9, ©shockpix.com/Alamy;
page 11, ©Blend Images/Alamy; pages 13, 25, 27, and 28, ©AP Photo; page 14, ©Roger
Hutchings/Alamy; page 17, ©iStockphoto.com/khuonghoang; page 19, ©Sveta San, used under
license from Shutterstock, Inc.; page 20, ©iStockphoto.com/zilli; page 21, ©Medical-on-Line/
Alamy; page 23, ©Pictorial Press Ltd/Alamy

Library of Congress Cataloging-in-Publication Data
Alter, Judith, 1938-
Vaccines / by Judith Alter.
    p. cm.–(Innovation in medicine)
ISBN-13: 978-1-60279-223-4
ISBN-10: 1-60279-223-2
1. Vaccines–Juvenile literature. 2. Vaccination–Juvenile literature.
I. Title. II. Series.
RA638.A49 2009
615'.372–dc22   2008002038

*Cherry Lake Publishing would like to acknowledge the work of
The Partnership for 21st Century Skills.
Please visit www.21stcenturyskills.org for more information.*

CONTENTS

Chapter One
Conquering a Dangerous Disease   **4**

Chapter Two
How to Deliver Vaccines   **9**

Chapter Three
Using Vaccines   **13**

Chapter Four
New Directions in Vaccines   **16**

Chapter Five
Some Famous Innovators   **21**

Glossary   30
For More Information   31
Index   32
About the Author   32

CHAPTER ONE

Conquering a Dangerous Disease

Children receive a number of vaccinations at various ages, usually beginning soon after they are born.

"Hurry up, Connie! We don't want to be late for your doctor's appointment," called Mom as she stepped into the garage.

"Why do I have to see the doctor? I'm not sick," complained Connie as she shut the garage door and climbed into the car. "She's just going to want to give me a bunch of shots. I don't like shots!"

"Those shots are part of the reason why you don't get sick very often," replied Mom.

"I don't get it. How can having a needle stuck in my arm keep me from getting sick? And who was crazy enough to start sticking needles into people's arms in the first place?" asked Connie.

"Good questions! I know a little bit about how vaccines prevent illness, but let's ask Dr. Bryant to explain how they work. Maybe she can even tell us who came up with the idea of vaccines."

✢ ✢ ✢

Vaccination or **immunization** protects the body against infection. It puts a harmless form of the germ that causes the disease into the system. Immunization triggers the body to activate its **immune system** and form **antibodies** to resist the disease.

People have long known that some diseases never infect a person twice. If you get the mumps, for instance, you will never get it again. The practice that we now call vaccination probably began in China centuries ago when people recognized

21st Century Content

Today, vaccines are used for more than 20 infectious diseases. Some vaccines are given only to people who have a high risk of being exposed to the disease. For example, if you're traveling to a country where typhoid fever is common and the disease is not found in your home country, you should probably receive a typhoid vaccine. Other vaccinations are recommended for everyone. On your immunization records, you might see "MMR" or "DTap." MMR is short for measles, mumps, and rubella. These three vaccines are given together in one shot. So are the vaccines for diphtheria, tetanus, and pertussis (known as DTaP). It's important to stay up-to-date on your vaccinations.

this principle. It was also practiced in many Middle Eastern countries.

Smallpox is the first disease that was successfully overcome with vaccination. Smallpox is a highly contagious infection caused by the variola (vair-ee-OH-luh) virus. A person with smallpox was spotted with small raised bumps that left bad scars.

A child receives a smallpox vaccination in a doctor's office in the 1870s.

Lady Mary Wortley Montagu of England saw children being vaccinated against smallpox when she traveled to Constantinople, Turkey, in the early 18th century. Montagu had smallpox as a child and insisted her own son be vaccinated. When she returned to England, she encouraged others to be **inoculated**.

English farmer Benjamin Jesty inoculated his wife and two sons for smallpox in 1774. But his method was different. He noticed that his milkmaids (the women he employed to milk dairy cows) nursed smallpox patients but never got sick themselves. The milkmaids, however, frequently had cowpox, a disease similar to smallpox but not as serious. He infected his family members with the cowpox virus, which gave them cowpox. Then they were able to avoid getting smallpox.

An English physician named Edward Jenner used a method he called variolation to prevent smallpox in his patients. This involved injecting a small amount of the variola virus into an opening in the skin of a patient. Some of his patients developed full cases of smallpox and died. Jenner noted that his patients who had cowpox in the past did not react to the variolation. He decided to test the idea that a person who has had cowpox could be immune to smallpox.

On May 14, 1796, Jenner inoculated young James Phipps with scrapings from the cowpox blister of a

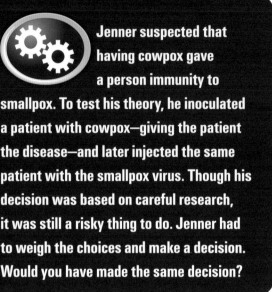

Learning & Innovation Skills

Jenner suspected that having cowpox gave a person immunity to smallpox. To test his theory, he inoculated a patient with cowpox—giving the patient the disease—and later injected the same patient with the smallpox virus. Though his decision was based on careful research, it was still a risky thing to do. Jenner had to weigh the choices and make a decision. Would you have made the same decision?

milkmaid. About a week later, the boy developed symptoms of cowpox. He had infected sores, chills, and head and body aches, and he lost his appetite. But he recovered quickly. After several weeks, Jenner exposed Phipps to the smallpox virus. Just as Jenner had guessed, Phipps didn't develop smallpox.

Jenner wrote about his method of vaccination. But other physicians doubted his findings. Then, in 1853, English law required that infants be vaccinated. Jenner's innovative thinking combined with research led to the protection of people against a serious disease. It taught the medical world much about disease prevention. Eventually, Jenner was recognized as the "father of modern vaccination."

Almost 200 years after Jenner's research, smallpox was no longer a threat worldwide. The last case in the United States was reported in 1949. The last naturally occurring case in the world was reported in 1977. In 1980, the World Health Organization officially declared that the world was free of smallpox.

CHAPTER TWO

How to Deliver Vaccines

The skin is a protective barrier for the body. It keeps germs and other harmful substances from entering the body. But it is also a barrier against medicines. Scientists and physicians had to solve the problem of how to get through that barrier to deliver vaccines.

Edward Jenner used a **lancet** to scratch two lines in James Phipps's skin. In the mid-1850s, the **hypodermic syringe**

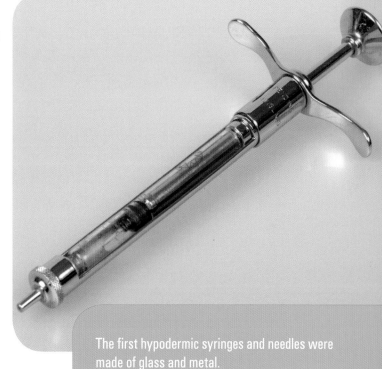

The first hypodermic syringes and needles were made of glass and metal.

became available. Early hypodermic needles were thick, which meant they caused painful injections. The needles could rust or snap in two. They were fitted to glass barrels that cracked, and they had tips that leaked. The needles had to be sharpened and **sterilized** before they could be used again.

Physicians also used vaccination, or vaccine, points. These were a lot like lancets. One end had a sharp point coated with the vaccine. Sometimes they were made of ivory or glass. The invention of the spring lancet eased patients' fears and discomfort. It shot the point quickly into the skin.

Sharpening and sterilizing needles between uses was time consuming. But it had to be done. If it wasn't, germs could be transferred from one patient to another. In the late 1940s and early 1950s, Dr. Arthur E. Smith worked at solving this problem. He created a disposable needle and syringe that was more convenient. In 1954, Becton, Dickenson and Company sold the first mass-produced disposable syringes and needles. This product was used to administer Dr. Jonas Salk's new **polio** vaccine to a million U.S. children.

In 1965, Benjamin Rubin developed a new needle design. He tried grinding down the center of the eye of a sewing needle. He kept refining his design and invented the bifurcated needle. This new kind of needle had two

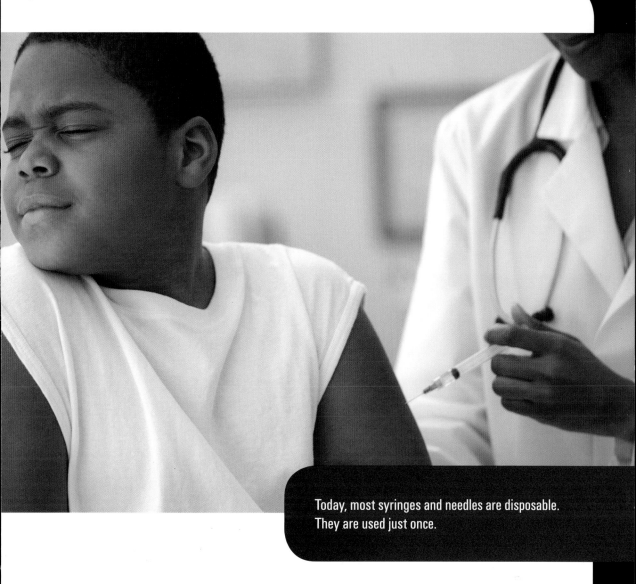

Today, most syringes and needles are disposable.
They are used just once.

thin points very close together. When dipped in the
vaccine, a small amount of the liquid clings between
the two points. Rubin's bifurcated needle was one of
the inventions that helped wipe out smallpox around
the world.

Learning & Innovation Skills

 In the United States, all children entering public or private schools are required to have some basic immunizations, including those for measles, mumps, and rubella. Some people oppose these requirements because they believe that the mercury used as a preservative in vaccines causes autism. Scientists have demonstrated that there is no connection between vaccines and autism. But the argument continues. Where would you go to find out more about this subject?

Researchers kept working to make needles that were less painful and more convenient to use. Microneedles were the next development. They are thinner and sharper and cause the patient less pain. In the early 21st century, prefilled, single-dose, disposable injection needles became common.

Some innovative thinkers wanted to find a way to deliver vaccines without having to inject patients. As a result of their work, a few vaccines are delivered by mouth or nasal sprays. These vaccines use weakened but active viruses. Viruses in shots are inactive.

CHAPTER THREE

Using Vaccines

The 1918 influenza **epidemic** killed between 20 million and 40 million people worldwide. This deadly outbreak traveled quickly and far. Some people think that conditions during and just after World War I (1914–1918) were responsible for the far-reaching effects of this epidemic. Soldiers' quarters were often overcrowded, making it easy for a disease to spread quickly. After

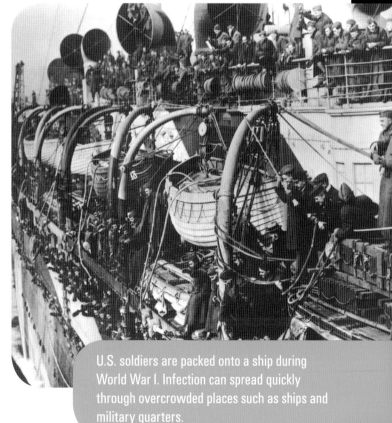

U.S. soldiers are packed onto a ship during World War I. Infection can spread quickly through overcrowded places such as ships and military quarters.

the war, soldiers returned to homes around the globe, bringing the influenza virus with them. Scientists realized the urgent need for vaccinating large populations of people living in places where it was easy to catch and spread diseases. During World War II (1939–1945), soldiers were vaccinated against typhus and tetanus, two diseases that are caused by bacteria.

Vaccine vials are often kept in ice packs before distribution. Many have labels that indicate whether they are still usable.

Large-scale vaccination programs present their own challenges. For large-scale vaccination programs to be effective, they must be affordable. Making, distributing, and giving vaccines all contribute to their cost. Vaccines have to be refrigerated, so storing them adds to the cost.

There are many children in the world whose families cannot afford vaccinations. It is estimated that 2 million children die every year from diseases, such as measles, that can be prevented with vaccines. Health care workers around the world are working on finding ways to make vaccines affordable and available to as many people as possible. Philanthropists (people who donate their money and time to help others) such as Bill and Melinda Gates are also joining in the fight.

21st Century Content

If vaccines are exposed to too much heat, they will spoil and have to be thrown out. Vaccine vial monitors (VVMs) were developed to detect whether or not a vaccine is still usable. These monitors, which are printed on the vial label or attached like stickers to the vial top, are heat sensitive. They start out light in color and darken as they are exposed to heat.

Introduced in 1996, VVMs have been used on nearly 2 billion vials. They have saved lives and money by keeping usable vaccines out of the trash. The World Health Organization estimates that the use of VVMs is saving the global health community at least $5 million every year.

CHAPTER FOUR

New Directions in Vaccines

What advances are scientists working on now? One is the development of vaccines that do not require refrigeration. This would make delivery of vaccines possible in isolated tropical climates. It would also decrease shipping and storage costs.

In addition, scientists are working on finding ways to give vaccines to people without using needles. They hope to develop more vaccines that can be taken by mouth. Patches that will deliver the vaccine through a patient's skin are another possibility. Mists or sprays that introduce vaccines through the nose are also being developed. A nasal spray form of the flu vaccine is already available. Some scientists are working to combine **genes** of a harmful disease agent with genes of edible plants—corn, potatoes, tomatoes, bananas, or lettuce. Then the food itself would be the vaccine.

One day, eating a banana might replace getting a shot for a vaccination. Vaccines might grow on trees!

Genetic engineering is one of the most exciting developments in vaccine research. Scientists have isolated the gene in some disease germs that signals the body to form specific antibodies. They can then inject just that

Learning & Innovation Skills

People around the world have been treating illnesses in a variety of ways for hundreds or even thousands of years. Some people practice homeopathy. This practice tries to activate the body's healing response with very small doses of substances that cause symptoms in a healthy person. This method is based on ideas similar to those that led to the development of vaccinations. Other alternative health practices include doing yoga and taking herbal remedies. Today, there is a trend to blend many different practices with commonly accepted modern medical care when treating patients. Many doctors now combine elements of these different practices to help their patients stay healthy, prevent illness, treat disease, and heal their bodies.

Do you think the doctors who bring together older and more modern forms of treatment should be considered innovators? Why or why not?

gene into patients, without injecting the whole germ. Such methods hold hope for preventing Lyme disease, malaria, and AIDS (a disease of the immune system).

Work continues for vaccines to prevent **avian flu**, and there is disagreement about the safety of an **anthrax** vaccine. Scientists are also working on vaccines to prevent addiction to tobacco and other drugs.

Some researchers are working on vaccines to treat and to prevent different types of cancer. Cancer is not caused by germs from outside the body. It is a group of body cells that multiply uncontrollably. Scientists hope to come up with a way to signal the cells to stop dividing. Such an innovation would help control the disease.

Sometimes new ideas come about by accident. For

Chickens crowd a commercial farm. Avian flu can spread quickly through populations of birds.

example, the vaccine to prevent tuberculosis (a disease that often affects the lungs) is sometimes effective in treating bladder cancer, but scientists aren't sure why. Further research may help uncover the link or lead to the discovery of new information. Then innovative researchers can come up with new ideas in their quest to conquer cancer.

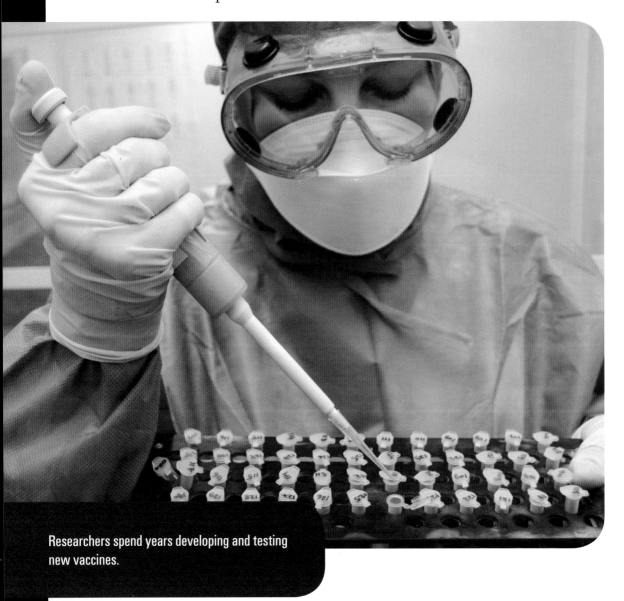

Researchers spend years developing and testing new vaccines.

CHAPTER FIVE

Some Famous Innovators

Although Edward Jenner is called the father of modern vaccination, many other scientists have played important parts. They have contributed to our understanding of how vaccines work and have developed vaccines themselves. French scientist Louis Pasteur researched the causes of diseases. The work of Jonas Salk,

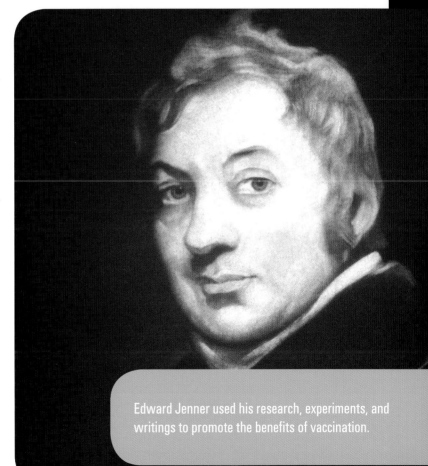

Edward Jenner used his research, experiments, and writings to promote the benefits of vaccination.

With the interests of the community in mind, Edward Jenner devoted his time to researching vaccines and studying patients. But that left him little time to practice medicine and earn a living. His commitment to helping others was recognized by the British Parliament when it awarded him 10,000 pounds in 1802 (about $500,000 in U.S. dollars) and an additional 20,000 pounds in 1807. He was also honored by Oxford, Harvard, and Cambridge universities.

Dr. Albert Sabin, and John Enders in the United States all contributed to stopping a polio epidemic.

Louis Pasteur and the Germ Theory of Disease

French scientist Louis Pasteur is best known for the germ theory of disease. Up until the 1880s, most scientists believed that diseases happened spontaneously. Nothing caused them—they just occurred. Pasteur proved that tiny organisms in the air or dirt, such as bacteria, cause disease. The process of pasteurization, which is named for him, is a way to remove bacteria from milk by boiling it and then cooling it. Milk that has been pasteurized doesn't go sour quickly. Today, most people drink only pasteurized milk.

By Pasteur's time, smallpox vaccination was common, thanks to Jenner's work. Pasteur took vaccination one step farther. He applied the technology to common diseases in animals and eventually to other diseases in humans.

Louis Pasteur proved that bacteria cause disease. The process of pasteurization is named for him.

Pasteur began doing research with chicken **cholera**. An assistant mistakenly let a culture of cholera sit too long before inoculating the chickens. The chickens developed some symptoms but did not die. In effect, they had been vaccinated with a weakened form of the bacteria. Pasteur observed this and then injected the chickens with fresh bacteria. They did not die. He realized they were immune.

Pasteur next applied this method to anthrax. He created an anthrax vaccine by exposing the disease-causing organism to oxygen. This weakened the disease. Pasteur used Jenner's term, vaccine, for all such products.

Pasteur's colleague, Emile Roux, had been developing a **rabies** vaccine by drying and preserving the spinal cords of infected rabbits. The vaccine had been tested only on 11 dogs when Pasteur applied it to a human patient. Nine-year-old Joseph Meister had been bitten by a rabid dog in 1885. At that time, a bite by or a scratch from a rabid animal was almost always deadly. Without the vaccine, the boy would surely die. But it was dangerous for Pasteur to administer the vaccine. He was not a licensed physician. If the boy developed rabies or died, Pasteur could be prosecuted for treating the boy. He administered the vaccine, and the boy did not develop rabies. Today, patients bitten by rabid animals can always be saved with rapid treatment.

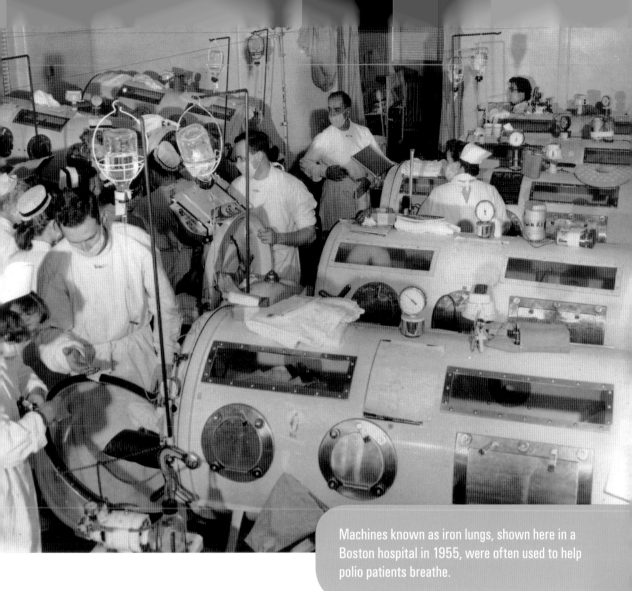

Machines known as iron lungs, shown here in a Boston hospital in 1955, were often used to help polio patients breathe.

Heroes of the Battle Against Polio

In the first half of the 20th century, Americans often spent their summers worrying about polio. Many believed that the danger of infection was greater in the city, so parents would send their children to the country in the summer. Parents believed if children got chilled in the water, they would develop polio, so swimming pools were often closed during outbreaks. Children feared polio, which was also known as infantile paralysis. They knew of people who had been crippled, even people who had to be in **iron lungs**.

In 1954, the president of the National Foundation for Infantile Paralysis (NFIP) estimated that in the coming summer 30,000 to 40,000 children would get polio. About 15,000 would be paralyzed and 1,000 would die. Today, polio is no longer a threat in the United States or much of the world, because of the polio vaccine.

Two men are known as the heroes in the battle against polio: Jonas Salk and Albert Sabin. But many scientists were racing to find a way to stop polio epidemics.

Jonas Salk developed a killed virus vaccine against all three strains, or types, of poliovirus. This type of vaccine uses a dead version of the virus. In 1952, he tested his vaccine on a small number of people, and it was successful. Two years later, Salk's team gave either the vaccine or a **placebo** to 1 million children, ages six to nine. Children had to be inoculated three times, once for each strain of the virus. Salk's vaccine did not give long-lasting immunity. Children had to have additional doses of the vaccine, known as booster shots. Also, it could only be given by injection.

Jonas Salk, seen here in his Pittsburgh laboratory, played a key role in the treatment of polio.

Albert Sabin developed a polio vaccine using weakened live virus. In the 1950s, he tested his vaccine on volunteer prisoners, his family, and himself. Sabin thought the live but weakened virus would provide longer immunity than the killed virus. The vaccine was taken by mouth, too, so people could avoid the dreaded shots.

In 1961, the Sabin live virus vaccine began to replace Salk's killed vaccine in the United States. For a few years, the two vaccines were given in alternating booster shots. Today in the United States, the Salk vaccine is used alone, though the Sabin vaccine is still used around the world.

Albert Sabin developed a polio vaccine that was taken by mouth, instead of being injected as a shot.

John Enders was overlooked in the publicity surrounding the development of polio vaccination. In 1948, he and colleagues Dr. T. H. Weller and Dr. F. C. Robbins demonstrated that the poliovirus could be grown in a laboratory. Until then, it was thought that the virus could be grown only in the brain or nervous system tissue of a live animal—making it impossible to develop a vaccine. The work of Enders and his colleagues laid the foundation for the development of the Salk and Sabin vaccines. Enders, Weller, and Robbins received the Nobel Prize for Physiology or Medicine in 1954 in recognition of their work.

Smallpox and polio are the great vaccine success stories. Others will come at a rapid rate as innovative thinkers continue to increase our knowledge of disease and the human body.

Glossary

anthrax (AN-thraks) an infectious disease that affects primarily cattle, sheep, and swine; it can also affect human beings; it is usually fatal

antibodies (AN-ti-bah-deez) disease-fighting proteins in the blood produced in response to the introduction of a specific threat

autism (AW-ti-suhm) a disorder of the brain that is characterized by difficulty communicating and forming relationships

avian flu (AY-vee-uhn FLOO) a virus that affects birds; in the 1990s, it was found to affect humans, although the risk is low

cholera (KAH-luh-ruh) an often deadly disease in which people experience vomiting, diarrhea, and great loss of fluids

epidemic (eh-puh-DEH-mik) an outbreak of disease that affects a large number of people in the same area at the same time

genes (JEENZ) parts of a cell that contain the information and instructions needed for the cell to function

hypodermic syringe (hye-puh-DUR-mik suh-RINJ) a glass, metal, or hard rubber tube that holds fluid to be injected; a hollow needle is fitted to it

immune system (ih-MYOON SISS-tuhm) the mechanism by which the body protects itself from disease

immunization (ih-myoo-nuh-ZAY-shun) act of making one resistant to a disease

inoculated (ih-NAH-kyuh-lay-ted) to receive the injection of a microorganism, especially in order to treat or prevent a disease

iron lungs (EYE-urn LUHNGZ) chamber-like machines that use pressure to simulate normal breathing when a patient cannot breathe on his or her own

lancet (LAN-set) small surgical instrument, usually double-edged and with a sharp point

placebo (pluh-SEE-boh) an inactive substance used in experiments; researchers can determine how effective a medication is by comparing the results for patients given the medication with those for patients given a placebo

polio (POH-lee-oh) short name for poliomyelitis, a disease that can cause paralysis

rabies (RAY-beez) a disease of the nervous system that is almost always fatal if untreated; humans are most often infected by the bite of an infected animal

sterilized (STEHR-uh-lyzd) made free from living microorganisms

For More Information

BOOKS

Collier, James Lincoln. *Vaccines*. New York: Benchmark Books, 2004.

Krohn, Katherine E. *Jonas Salk and the Polio Vaccine*. Mankato, MN: Capstone Press, 2007.

Wells, Ken R., ed. *Vaccines*. Detroit: Greenhaven Press, 2007.

WEB SITES

KidsHealth for Kids—Vaccine
www.kidshealth.org/kid/word/v/word_vaccine.html
Learn more about vaccines and keeping yourself healthy

U.S. Food and Drug Administration: All about Vaccines
www.fda.gov/oc/opacom/kids/html/vaccines.htm
Learn the facts about vaccines and their importance

Index

anthrax, 18, 24
antibodies, 5, 18
autism, 12

bacteria, 14, 22, 24
Becton, Dickenson and
    Company, 10
bifurcated needles, 10–11
booster shots, 26, 28

cancer, 18, 19–20
cholera, 24
cost, 15, 16
cowpox, 7, 8

diphtheria, 5

Enders, John, 22, 29
epidemics, 13–14, 22,
    25–26

foods, 16–17

Gates, Bill, 15
Gates, Melinda, 15
genetic engineering,
    17–18

germs, 5, 9, 10, 17–18, 22
germ theory, 22

history, 5–8, 9, 10–12
homeopathy, 18
hypodermic syringes,
    9–10. See also needles.

immune system, 5, 18
immunization, 5, 12
infantile paralysis. See
    polio.
influenza, 13–14, 16
iron lungs, 26

Jenner, Edward, 7–8, 9,
    21, 22, 24
Jesty, Benjamin, 7

lancets, 9, 10
laws, 8

measles, 5, 12, 15
Meister, Joseph, 24
mercury, 12
microneedles, 12

Montagu, Lady Mary
    Wortley, 7
mumps, 5, 12

nasal sprays, 12, 16
National Foundation
    for Infantile Paralysis
    (NFIP), 26
needles, 10–12, 16.
    See also hypodermic
    syringes.
Nobel Prize, 29

pasteurization, 22
Pasteur, Louis, 21, 22, 24
pertussis, 5
philanthropists, 15
Phipps, James, 7–8, 9
polio, 10, 22, 25–29

rabies, 24
refrigeration, 15, 16
risk, 5, 8
Robbins, F. C., 29
Roux, Emile, 24
rubella, 5, 12
Rubin, Benjamin, 10, 11

Sabin, Albert, 22, 26,
    27–28, 29
Salk, Jonas, 10, 21–22,
    26, 28, 29
smallpox, 6–8, 11, 22, 29
Smith, Arthur E., 10
syringes. See hypodermic
    syringes.

tetanus, 5, 14
travel, 5, 13–14
tuberculosis, 19–20
typhus, 14

vaccination programs, 15
vaccine points, 10
vaccine vial monitors
    (VVMs), 15
variolation, 7
variola virus, 6, 7

Weller, T. H., 29
World Health Organization,
    8, 15
World War I, 13
World War II, 14

About the Author

Judy Alter grew up in Chicago in the 1950s and remembers the summer polio scares and the relief that the discovery of the vaccine brought. The director of Texas Christian University Press, she is the author of numerous books for both children and adults. She is the mother of four and grandmother of seven. Ms. Alter lives in Fort Worth, Texas, with her dog and cat.